Re:*VITAL*ize

Your Church Through
Gospel Recovery

Alvin L. Reid

Gospeladvance books

advancing a gospel movement in all of life

Dedicated to those who endure

Alvin L. Reid

CONTENTS

Foreword

There is a cry coming from the established church that we must not ignore: "What are we going to do about the overwhelming needs of the plateaued and declining churches?" The statistics indicate that we have an epidemic on our hands. We must address this question of church health.

If you lead a church that needs revitalizing, and are not looking for gimmicks or a quick fix, you may be looking for someone who understands your situation—someone with fresh ideas and experience. Alvin Reid is a man of God with that fresh yet experienced voice. Dr. Reid is a passionate practitioner who loves the local church. He has taught scores of pastors and church leaders in his classes. He has traveled extensively and knows what is happening in churches big and small. Pouring his scholarship through a heart of love, Alvin's authenticity positions him to be a unique voice that crosses generational lines, challenges thinking, and encourages hearts.

In this book, Alvin talks straight about church health in the light of Scripture. He compares church health to a healthy functioning body and uses examples from church history to shine fresh light on the subject. He has a special ability to weave all of these together and provide a collection of insights, illustrations, and tools for the journey.

Don't get in a hurry. Read a little—pray a lot. Read some more—pray some more. Let it soak in—then live it out! Join me in praying for a movement of Gospel recovery through revitalization and a multiplied Gospel presence through church planting. Christ deserves both....

"...to Him be glory in the church and in Christ Jesus to all generations, forever and ever. Amen" Eph. 3:21

H. Al Gilbert
Vice-President for Evangelism, North American Mission Board, SBC

Acknowledgements

Over the years I have had the honor of preaching in thousands of churches. Many of these stand in need of a fresh work of God, a revitalizing work. This book hopes to offer encouragement and some guidance for those who seek to lead such a work of revitalization.

Many have helped me in this process, and no doubt I will leave out numerous names that have shaped me, and thus my thoughts in this book. In particular I want to thank my president Danny Akin for his love for the local church and the gospel. Faithful pastors, from Johnny Hunt and J.D. Greear, who have led revitalizing works on a mammoth scale, as well as pastors Chris Crain and Randy Alston, and others have helped me to offer advice from men on the front lines of ministry.

Several people read this and gave me helpful comments, including Al Gilbert, who wrote the Foreword, John Mark Harrison, Don McCutcheon, Jared Johnson, and Bobby Gettys. My secretary Peggy Loafman helped as well in the process of preparing this. Our daughter Hannah helped to produce the logo for Gospel Advance Books, for which this book is the first of many to come (www.gospeladvancebooks.com). Bailey Shoemaker and Tim Jones created the cover. I thank God for gifted, creative people.

Any shortcomings of this book are mine.

Introduction

"A year from now you will wish you had started today." Karen Lamb

This past year I took up golfing with vigor. For about three months. About the same time I began playing in earnest I also began to experience numbness in my legs. My wife observed the numbness coincided with my renewed involvement in golfing. After a couple of visits to doctors, I landed in the office of a back specialist who explained the problem: spinal stenosis.

He sent me to physical therapy where I met a delightful Australian physical therapist named Murray. Murray put me on an exercise regimen with one simple goal: to activate my transverse abdominal muscles in order to relieve the pressure in my lumbar area so I would be able to walk again without the numbness. I had actually been in physical decline for years in this area of my anatomy; even significant weight loss and exercise regimen had missed this problem.

My body needed to be revitalized. And this is the case of many local churches, each an example of the Body of Christ. The New Testament refers to the church as the body of Christ often (see for instance Romans 12:3-5; I Corinthians 12:12-26; Ephesians 1:22-23, 5:25-32; Colossians 1:17-20, 3:14-16). Studies indicate the vast majority of our churches exhibit a spiritual form of unhealthiness not unlike an ailing body. For some, a diet of watered-down theology or pragmatism has led to a malnourished body; some need a realignment to the purposes of God; others need a serious visit to a spiritual eye doctor to get a renewed vision for what their church should be and could become. For many, a gradual, almost unnoticeable slide into stagnation is the culprit. Somewhere along the way the story and the glory of the gospel in all of life became replaced with the religious activities and preferences of church members.

I hope in this simple book to offer both a diagnosis and a prescription for churches and leaders who are sick and tired of being sick and tired, who want to replace the status quo with Great Commission effectiveness. More than anything I hope to encourage leaders – pastors, members, young and old – to settle neither for the status quo nor for simply moving somewhere else to start afresh in ministry. I want to challenge you to stay where you are, seek the face of God, stand on the unchanging gospel, and see God move afresh. Across America we have thousands of churches capable of beginning again to serve God with a passion; they need a fresh wind of the Spirit with leadership to teach and to model for them the vitality of the gospel. I hope to encourage you to be one of those churches pursuing renewal, revitalization, and God willing, deep and gospel-rich revival.

Where is your church? Are you a vibrant body of Christ, racing forward for the glory of God and busy about the gospel? Or, do you demonstrate symptoms of stagnation or decline? Has your growth been stunted? Do you function weekly as the people of God in your community, but at the same time does it seems as though a sort of numbness toward the gospel, toward the lost, maybe even toward one another exists? Has apathy replaced passion? Over the past ten years what has been the gospel trajectory of your congregation?

> I hope to encourage you to be one who pursues renewal, revitalization, and God willing, deep and gospel-rich revival.

Church planting has received significant attention in recent years. I thank God for this. I teach and/or mentor more than a few planters these days. We *need* many new churches. We need your church to help plant churches, and that may in fact help to revitalize it. But I also have a great burden for the multiple thousands of churches who have lost their vigor, who seem as it were to do what must be done to get by more than passionately running hard after Christ.

Such churches seem to be more effective at perpetuating strife than proclaiming salvation. Things must change. And they can.

> If you are interested in getting your church involved in planting see what the North American Mission Board of the Southern Baptist Convention is doing here: http://www.namb.net/Involving_My_Church/

My physical therapist told me the most important thing I could do in my condition was to *activate* my transverse abdominal muscles, because when I do I take pressure off my spine and move it to the muscles in the front which were created to bear the weight. In other words, I needed to help my body get back to functioning as it was created. If the situation became more serious I would need a more radical treatment, including potential back surgery. If I got my abs working better my back would have less pressure, with the overall impact greater health.

Some churches recline in a deathbed state so near to spiritual death they need to be replanted, virtually starting over. Nothing less than radical spiritual surgery will do. But most do not sit at death's door; they need a renewed vision to live consistently with the mission of God found in the Bible, not to be put into spiritual traction.

We have the resources in our churches to see a revitalized body. We have the Word of God to teach us. We have the Holy Spirit to serve as our Divine physical therapist to take us to new levels of health and vitality. We have the power of prayer. We have the gospel. And we have opportunities all around us to see God working.

We need to see the indicative of the gospel as well as the imperative, or to understand both the why and the how of change. When all you do is focus on the how, you will rarely see long-term change, preferring to find the quick fix, the program, or the magic bullet. In a world of fast food, microwaves, and social media we can forget that some changes take more than an email or a download.

Why do so many churches need revitalization? Our churches teem with believers who do what they do because this is what they were taught: show up in church, be faithful in attendance, be moral, but don't get terribly excited about all this. Raise children who love Jesus: children who don't get into trouble, get a good education and good jobs, and fit into society well. Just don't get too crazy about Jesus. Between a lack of vision for the gospel and people on the one hand and the impact of the idols of our time (leisure, consumerism, self-indulgence, etc.) we have gradually stopped running the race and find ourselves too often limping along half numbed.

But those who led remarkable times of revitalization and revival had a more radical view of Christianity. John Wesley led a movement that changed history in England. He said "Give me 100 men who fear nothing but God and hate nothing but sin, and I care not a straw whether they be clergy or lay, I will storm the gates of hell and set up the kingdom of God on earth."

Mark Twain's definition of a church: A good person talking to good people about how good they are.

Most churches have many people who really love Jesus. But too many do not see the reason for the malaise in their lives and in their church; like a person aware of some physical ailment, they know something is awry, but either will not or do not know how to change. It is the role of the leader to serve as the physician to diagnose the issues biblically and to help activate their faith in the same way my physical therapist helped me to activate my muscles. This must not include only a series of exercises, because the effort required to do the exercises must be motivated to carry out the rigorous work required. This requires a comprehensive approach.

Could it be that your greatest days are yet ahead? I have been in a few churches over the years that saw a fresh wind of God and a renewed passion birthed. In every case the leaders of the church were the most broken, the most focused, the most hungry for a work of God. Do you remember a time when you led the church of God with greater passion? Do you recall a burden to love God and love people no matter what?

Pastor Johnny Hunt of the First Baptist Church of Woodstock, Georgia, a remarkable example of a revitalized church, offers conferences on revitalization with the North American Mission Board. Check out this ministry here: http://www.namb.net/church-revitalization-video/

Remember this: revitalization is a *process, not an event.* You will not likely see a dramatic change in your church with a big event. The right events tied to a longer process can help, but events can get in the way of a process of revitalization because they mask long term change needed in the short-term successes of events.

Remember also: revitalization is a *process, not a program.* There is no magic bullet, no simple fix, no eight-steps to forever change. Despite all the fads and infomercials promising painless solutions to obesity, the truth is that if you are seriously out of shape, it will take time and a lot of effort to change. You will have to stop eating junk food and living like you are entitled to feed yourself garbage. Like events, programs can help, but also like events they can cloud the real need for change with short-term excitement or involvement. We often settle for a good event or a good program while ignoring the long-term change needed to bring deeper and longer changes, just like junk food fills the stomach briefly but does not help the body over time.

Be encouraged! Just like long term changes for one's health may make less visible changes in the short term but offer substantive changes as one's lifestyle changes, a long term commitment to a revitalized church takes longer but is worth it! I know of a pastor who labored in India for 16 years with little visible fruit. Now, his ministry plants thousands of churches. I know a pastor of a large church in the U.S. whose church puttered along for a decade but then grew significantly the following decade both numerically and spiritually. Think less of a fad diet and more of a lifestyle change to see lasting fruit.

The following offers a journey to see afresh the God Who is vital, active, at work in our time. Revitalizing a church does not start with a list of how to's, but with a fresh vision of God and His Lordship over the church. What do I mean by revitalization? Here is what I don't mean.

--Restoring the church to her "glory" days. First, they may not be as glorious as you recall. But more importantly, Christianity is an advancing movement, always hoping, seeking, and longing for more of God and His work in His people. Pastors I meet whose churches are revitalized tend to be grateful for all God has done and yet never satisfied with where they are.

--Simply following a formula guaranteed to revitalize. If God does not do it, it will not happen. Can you see signs of God's work? My friend J.D. Greear, lead pastor of the Summit Church in Raleigh-Durham, saw almost four years of winnowing, refocusing, and preparing the church before he led them to an explosion of growth. We all want revitalization, but will we endure the years of preparation?

Ligon Duncan, former head of the Presbyterian Church in America denomination, said that "Pastors consistently *over*estimate what they can accomplish in 5 years; they consistently *under*estimate what they accomplish in 20 years."

--Numerical growth only. For a church to be truly revitalized she may actually go through a decline at first. Revitalization means a serious return to the Lord of the Church, and that may well include some pruning. And, when revitalization comes, there are varying levels of growth and various types of growth. If you simply grow because you figure out a way to host events that make a splash in town you may get some numbers, but the reality of the refocusing of your church will be seen more in the local restaurants and neighborhoods, schools and businesses than a simple numbers game on Sundays. You will not only measure the number of *seats* filled on Sundays but also the number of believers who live *sent* lives daily.

Many churches can return to a focus on the glory of God. Revitalization refers to a recapturing of the mission of God as seen in Scripture to be the people of God living on mission regardless of vocation or location. And it emphasizes what we see the Bible affirms and what all people seek. Revival, the movement of God to awaken His people and transform a region (or more) for His glory, is the need of the hour. But as we pray for revival, let us be faithful to seek to become all He calls us to be. And, perhaps He will even trust us enough to send a fresh wind of His Spirit.

Each of the following chapters includes three practical helps: First, an example of a church that experienced revitalization from a spiritual awakening in history. Second, I give you a book to offer further material about the topic of that chapter. My students learn that most of the time when they ask me a question I reply with a book to read. Finally, I offer a "Take Action" section to use with leaders or a small group to make further application.

The next five chapters focus on specific areas that lead to a revitalized church following the acrostic VITAL:

Vision: See and recover the gospel.

Ingestion: Feed yourself and your people on the Word with gospel eyes.

Traction: Get moving by stepping out of the church building into missional living.

Alignment: Lead your church to line up everything she is about with clear standards.

Leverage: Be encouraged by others.

But there is a final word at the outset that is the most important word. None of these will matter without prayer. I know of no church that saw a revitalizing movement without deep, intense prayer. I know of no revival movement that happened without deep, fervent prayer. If you choose between spending time praying and reading this book, stop reading and start praying. But if you choose to read this, please do so in a spirit of earnest, continuous prayer. Ask God to give you wisdom. Ask God to fuel your passion. Ask God to give you a relentless desire to sacrifice everything for His glory. Then, when revitalization comes, you will know it was His work.

Because it is.

Chapter One
GOSPEL VISION: A Vision of God and for
Gospel Recovery

If you want to build a ship, don't drum up people together to collect wood and don't assign them tasks and work, but rather teach them to long for the endless immensity of the sea."

Antoine de Saint Exupery

I played high school football. I have a scar on my knee as a daily reminder. Back then I liked to think of myself as agile, mobile, and hostile, but today I am fragile, senile, and docile! I still love football. I love to watch it, that is.

You take very little risk by watching a football game compared to playing in a game. You can work up your emotions and get a little stressed, and you might trip over the coffee table if you get really carried away. Your greatest danger is in the junk food you eat while watching. Watching football is a lot safer than playing it in full gear. But one can hardly get in the kind of shape that marks an athlete by watching games from the comfort of one's living room, and the thrill of being on a team far surpasses the couch potato experience.

How does one activate the faith of believers in a church that resembles a spiritual couch potato? How do we help them to stand on the promises of God daily instead of simply sitting on the premises of the church building weekly? I meet so many leaders who fret over the apathy of their church — why the apathy, given we have such an amazing Lord to serve? The change starts with seeing things clearly as they are. Only then can we forge a new story, a new beginning.

A few years ago I recorded a video series on parenting. Before previewing it for a class I decided to pop in the VD and give it a look. I sat stunned at how overweight I looked. I had never seen myself as overweight, but that was in fact me on the screen, and I could not deny it. I looked overweight because I was overweight! I thought of those days playing high school football where our coach showed us the film from the previous week. "The big eye doesn't lie," he would say. I took some measurements and was sadly convinced that I was in a most pathetic state. The negative reality awakened me. But there was more.

I had recently purchased an amazon kindle and had (for what reason I have no idea) bought a book by a man in his 60s on fitness. He argued winsomely that the idea of having a healthy body in the 20s but not in the 60s was nonsense. He gave me positive hope.

I received both a negative shock and positive hope. But that was still not enough. I had to get back to the WHY. Why should it matter what I weighed, and why should it matter about my physical body as long as my quiet time was consistent? I did not need to be an athlete to teach classes, write, or preach, so why challenge the status quo? Because of the gospel, I realized. In I Corinthians 6:20 Paul writes: "for you were bought with a price, therefor glorify God with your body." Jesus' work on the cross serves as a motivation to care for our body. The immediate context had to do with abstaining from immorality, but the larger point of caring for our bodies in all ways applies as well.

As a follower of Christ I had to come back to the truth that my physical body belongs to Christ. I have been called to glorify God not only in explicitly "spiritual" ways, but also with my body. For the body of Christ to yearn for revitalization it must begin with the truth that she does not exist for herself or for her members, but she belongs to God. We cannot compartmentalize the local church any more than we can compartmentalize ourselves. The center of the local church is neither the pastor nor the people. The center is Christ.

The negative thought of being overweight made me feel bad, but it did not make me change. The positive hope that I could be in better shape encouraged me, but it did not move me to action. Only when I reflected on the work of Christ, and from that thought of the influence He has given me as a minister of the gospel and a teacher, was my faith activated to change. I want to finish well, and run the race as long as I can. And, the inner drive within me, the burden Christ put in me to matter for Him, to fulfill my calling well, drove me to change.

For us to be renewed as a church we must see two things very clearly. **First, we must see what does not change**: the Word of God and the gospel it proclaims, and the mission of God it calls us to live. Jesus is the point, not us. These are not negotiable. **Second, we must see where we are at this place and time in history, and seek to live and proclaim the gospel of the Kingdom effectively in our time.**

"When there are challenges to the status quo, those challenges must still "articulate" with the social setting." That is, an alternative vision of society-its discourse, moral demands, institutions, symbols, and rituals-must still resonate closely enough with the social environment that it is plausible to people. If it does not, the challenge will be seen as esoteric, eccentric, parochial, and thus either unrealistic or irrelevant. On the other hand, if the challenge articulates too closely with the social environment that produces it, the alternative will likely be co-opted by that which it seeks to challenge and change."[i] James Davidson Hunter

In other words, if you are one step ahead you are a leader, but if ten steps ahead you are an idiot.

Similarly, two things must happen in a church for her to change. **First, the church must want to change.** If there is a satisfaction with the status quo, a love for the current "fellowship" over reaching the lost, and a greater hunger for preferences in corporate worship than a yearning for the mission, then the church has misplaced passions. Prayer and ministry of the Word over time can change this, but unless this changes the idea of revitalization is just that, an idea. But even wanting to change will not bring change. **The church must also be willing to pay the *price* of**

change. Most church members would argue that they desire to change, to grow, to honor the Lord. But fewer will move to pay the price necessary. But here is the good news: when the leadership of the church –the pastor, staff, key leaders among the membership—genuinely desire to change and are willing to change no matter the cost, there is great hope for that church to become once again the people of God on mission for God.

A Biblical Focus, Not a Tangent

In Acts 1:8 Jesus gives with great clarity both the mission (witnesses unto Jesus) and the power to complete the mission (the Spirit). He further gives an effective strategy (Jerusalem, Judea, and so on). The book of Acts unfolds the early believers' story in which they took the unchanging message and shared it both by word and deed with remarkable effect, even in the face of great difficulty. Paul personified this when he wrote the Romans, telling them he not only hoped to come there, but to go toward "the ends of the earth" in Spain as well.

These early believers were quite aware of their need for God. They spent days praying for power. The leaders kept their focus on the Word and prayer, knowing that to lose focus on those would lead to peril. But they adapted the unchanging message and applied it in various ways.

In Acts 2, the early believers (all of them, see 2:10-11) shared a vision for gospel impact, intentionally sharing the good news with fellow Jews. Peter's message in Acts 2 offers Jesus as the Messiah for whom the Jews sought. This was a beautiful picture of applying a timeless gospel in a timely manner. In Acts 17 at Mars Hill, the apostle Paul spoke to Greeks, not Jews. He never mentioned a Messiah, for they sought none. He did speak of creation, and the great drama of the gospel, and applied the gospel to their idolatry. He did so because his audience changed, though the gospel does not.

We can be sincere, and we can believe the gospel, and still be very ineffective. I meet people in church after church who talk to me about people they know, especially young people, who are not being reached by their church. They understand something must change but often do not understand what is required to change. Why have so many churches become ineffective.

Many today have taken one part of the Bible and built their version of the gospel around a tangent:

--The Bible speaks of prosperity, but some take that and create a "prosperity gospel" that denies the biblical gospel;

--The Bible has many commands, but some take the commands and create a legalistic system that loses the gospel in moralisms, creating modern-day Pharisees rather than servants of God;

--The Bible speaks of miracles, so some take that teaching and apply it to everything, creating a culture that elevates physical miracles above the atoning work of Christ.

Today there is a growing recovery of the gospel in its robust, whole-Bible understanding. More and more books about the gospel are being written, and more talk about the great metanarrative of Scripture, that the whole Bible really has one central Story of a redeeming God. Helping believers to see afresh the wonder and the glory of the Story of God's redemption in Jesus must be central to any vision of revitalization.

Recent books on the gospel:
J.D. Greear. *Gospel.*
Matt Chandler with Jared Wilson, *Explicit Gospel.*
Jared Wilson. *Gospel Wakefulness.*
Greg Gilbert. *What Is the Gospel?*
John Piper. *God Is the Gospel.*
Scott McKnight. *The King Jesus Gospel.*

A Renewed Vision

Several years ago I went to the eye doctor because I had trouble when reading things up close. He prescribed bifocals. I did not like to admit I was getting older and needed to change. But listening to the doctor and heeding his prescription led to improved vision and overall health for my eyes. Like a man whose eyes gradually weaken over time, it often takes an outside diagnosis, or a crisis – a financial issue, a change in leadership, or some other factor -- for believers to see their church with honest eyes.

I will never forget a student who took a church growth class I taught. He just knew his church was a vibrant model of growth. And, the church had shown healthy growth in the past. But when he tracked the previous five years he found a church on a trajectory of significant decline. The reality failed to match his perception.

The worst thing you as a leader can do is chastise the members for being in a declining church, and the second worst thing is to take all the blame yourself and live a defeated life. Most of the members are living out the Christianity they have been taught and had modeled by years of church leaders. They can change, and you can be part of the change.

Look at these simple statistics in your church, tracking the past five years:

--Baptisms: how many have you baptized annually the past five years?

--Sunday school/small group attendance.

--Worship attendance.

--Number of believers actively involved in the community for the sake of the gospel: volunteering, serving in the local schools, adopting restaurants or neighborhoods for ministry focus, and so on.

--Number of believers annually involved in mission trips both national and international.

What is the trajectory shown over the past five years? While these numbers can serve as part of a set of "vital signs" (like body temperature, blood pressure, etc.), they can at times be deceiving. Using only metrics like these can fail to see deeper issues at work either positively or negatively. My wife Michelle suffered from fatigue and other issues for many years. She had a basic test for Lyme disease, which had been negative. But another doctor years later put her through a more thorough battery of tests. She did have the disease, and after a fairly grueling treatment regimen is healthier today than she had been in years! If we only treat surface issues in a dying church we are like a decorator who changes the curtains in a house crumbling down.

Other questions to consider:

--What is the attitude of my church among waiters and waitresses and others in the service industries in your area? Some churches are woefully infamous for the terrible treatment of servers. What about the police? Firefighters? While unscientific, this can give you some idea as to whether your church is beloved (or even known) in your community. This can give some insight into whether you are a gospel community advancing the mission or an introverted proponent of the Christian subculture. News travels through many communities through the restaurants and through those who protect us. If the members of your church regularly stiff the waiters and show no care for them, believe me, people will know.

--What is the impact of our church in the public schools in the area? Public schools offer one of the great mission fields in our day.

--In times of crisis in the community do those outside your church look to you for help?

--Ask this question of your church: how many of you grew up in a Christian home (it is normally 80-90%)? Then ask, how many of you have talked as a family about reaching out to your neighbors (in my experience with plateaued or declining churches, you will get about a 10% response). Don't scold the people at that point, because they do not talk to their neighbors because they have never been shown, taught, and released to do so by their church leaders in most cases. But this simple test can help you to see where your church is in terms of understanding a missional life (more on that later).

--Ask the people in the church on a given Sunday to write down the names of people they know in the community who do not know Christ. Collect those names. If they turn in far more names than the number of people there on that

Sunday you have a church aware of the lost around them. But in most plateaued or declining churches you will get far less names than the number of people turning in those names. This is a simple way of determining how the members think about the people around them from the viewpoint of gospel eyes.

--Look at the past several copies of your weekly bulletin or worship folder. How much of the print there is focused on maintaining the status quo or getting people into the church building weekly? On the other hand, how much attention is given to living out the gospel daily in the community? We promote what we most care about.

Before a doctor can prescribe change through medicine or therapy he must first diagnose the issue. In the same way, before we can have a fresh vision for a revitalized church we must diagnose the issues that keep up from effective ministry. This involves two specific areas: how we relate to the culture outside the church, and how we understand the purpose within the church.

Understand Our Culture

Part of the reason for the malaise in the church comes from the changes in our culture. Our world has changed dramatically, and sometimes churches are slow to adapt, leading to stagnation.

Over a century ago the Industrial Revolution led to **Mass production** as large factories drew people to cities. Henry Ford and others after him perfected the assembly line and the capacity to make large numbers of products en masse. This reality and the rapid urbanization of the times matched perfectly with the most effective tool of evangelism in the latter 19th and early 20th century: the mass urban meeting. D. L. Moody pioneered this approach that was followed by a phalanx of evangelists: Billy Sunday, Wilbur Chapman, Mordecai Ham, and others. While Ford mass produced his automobiles, the church witnessed mass conversions in these meetings.

In the middle of the twentieth century we saw the rise

of **mass media**. The television escalated this shift, making advertisers grow in influence. "Try this product;" "use this brand," we were told. It was the day of the Fuller Brush salesman going door to door with his prepackaged sales pitch. At this time we saw the rise of programmatic approaches to ministry in the church, including packaged evangelism training. The Church Growth Movement arose as well, offering specialists to help diagnose issues and offer processes for change. This proved to be as effective in this era for a time as mass crusades had been previously.

During this time the Sunday school became a dominant force in church life as a part of the larger programmatic focus. Sunday school had existed long before, but in the latter half of the 20th century books, conferences, and programs focusing on growing the church through the Sunday school became a significant feature of the church landscape.

But times have changed again. We have moved from a mass production age to a mass media era to **the information age**. The Internet has changed everything. This has led to our time currently in which ideas rule the day, and especially ideas that are spread through stories. Look at the television today and see the infomercials using testimonies and note the reality shows in which your neighbor could be a star. As I write this a recent winner of American Idol, Scotty McCreery, sat in a youth group in a church where I preached just across town from my home only three years ago.

Add to that the sudden ascension of social media as the dominant force on the Internet (it now outranks porn as #1 online). Everyone has an idea today, it seems. And, individuals can have great influence, whether it is a Justin Bieber who got his start not by signing with a record label but by posting on YouTube (I'm not a fan, I'm just illustrating), or the founders of Craigslist or Wikipedia, our day is a day of community (with Third Places like Starbucks), ideas, and stories.

This is why I have personally seen more people, many very unchurched or dechurched, come to Christ by sharing the gospel from the perspective of the whole Bible. I use The Story (www.viewthestory.com), explaining creation, fall, rescue through Christ alone, and restoration. The churches I observe who need revitalization have tended to reduce the gospel to the most brief and simple of presentations possible and tend to share the gospel as briefly as possible with people they hardly know and through big events with evangelists. For some in their practice the gospel becomes a means to get people out of hell more than how to know God. When we do the bare minimum of gospel work over time, even people in the church begin to perceive it not as the central principle that changes all of life: relationships, economics, etc. Instead, people begin to see it as one more religious practice we do on our way to live as religious consumers.

Today many unchurched and dechurched young adults come to Christ through personal relationships, and in particular small groups meeting in homes. Third places where stories can be shared in an informal and safe space appeal to people today. The shift to Starbucks as a meeting site for businesses and such technologies as Go To Meeting and Regus office space that can be rented as needed has shifted the workforce increasingly from a centralized building to a more mobile approach. Multisite churches and small groups in homes have replaced the gymnasiums/family life centers and education buildings built by the last generation. In other words, if we will be serious about revitalizing, we have to move the center of our outreach from the church building to the culture. In Acts, 39 of the 40 miracles recorded happened outside the gathered church. Today we can expect to see a more vital Christianity as we see its effect in the community.

Seeing Clearly Within the Church Body

Many churches still use the mass event and programmatic approaches to reach a culture that has to no small degree left those behind. Certainly some can still have effective mass events; I'm not at all arguing we should cease to have them. But the tool of events can no longer be the template for our ministry. Many churches still effectively use the Sunday school. If your church is a Sunday school focused church I would not suggest that the first thing you do to revitalize is to dismantle the Sunday school (that might be the last thing you do as a pastor at that church!). I am simply submitting that to have a revitalized church today we need to see the church and our ministries less as a factory appealing to mass crowds, or a program-creating institution, which leads to an overemphasis on getting people into a building on Sundays, and more as the body of Christ investing on a much more personal level, telling the Story of the gospel and showing its change in everyday life as we live in the culture. We have to be honest about our preferences and distinguish them from unchanging truth. This will take time, but is a journey worth investing your life.

A church must move from preferences, even preferences that have been good and successful in the past, to practices that are both biblical and effective. If your church offered a dramatic presentation at Christmas that reached people for years, but in all honestly has not reached many in more recent years, there is no justification for continuing the status quo just because people in the church still enjoy doing it.

I often talk with pastors who struggle with a church that needs revitalizing. Just yesterday I spoke with a student from one of the oldest, most historic churches in the Southern Baptist Convention. And, he would argue, one of the most dead spiritually. I reminded him that the institutionalism and obsession with the past and tradition so characteristic of his church was so because they people in that church were simply doing what they had been taught to do. In past efforts to care for believers and reach the lost, so much attention was given to the forms – Sunday school, key programs and ministries that fit pervious times – that to change the forms would seem to many to be an attack of the Bible. So one of the most important roles of a leader of revitalization is to help people see the difference between the mission of God in Scripture -- which does not change -- and the forms we use which can and often must change. The unintended consequence of a very successful era of Sunday school and of institutional-focused Christianity has been a compartmentalization of the faith into those times we are zealous for God (i.e. when in the church building) instead of seeing life as worship and life as a daily mission trip.

An Example of a Church's Renewed Vision: Richard Baxter

A significant example of a revitalized church of when the believers there recaptured a vision for the message of the gospel and the mission of God occurred in London in 1665. Shortly before the renewal ignited, the plague ravaged the city. In one week ten thousand died. "Many who were in church one day, were thrown into the grave the next," wrote Gillies.[ii]

As preachers proclaimed God's Word, the churches overflowed as people crowded one another just to hear the message of eternal life. The people did not know if they would be alive the next day. A sense of urgency fuels a revitalized church.

As the preachers preached the redemptive message of Christ, they were marked by urgency and compassion. This was no day for Sunday-only Christianity. Nor is our day! The words of Richard Baxter, "I preach as a dying man to dying men"[iii] characterized their labors. The people grasped for the Word of God as a drowning man sought to catch a rope. As the scourge overwhelmed the city the subject of eternity grew in importance. "Ministers were sent to knock, cry aloud, and lift up their voice like a trumpet" said Gillies, "Then the people began to open the ear and the heart, which were fast shut and barred before; how they did hearken, as for their lives, as if every sermon were their last."[iv]

Facing the possibility of death, thousands responded to the message of Christ. People desperately sought for answers, came under conviction, and were converted. The death rate caused believers to live out the mission of God with great urgency and at risk. This revival in the midst of a crisis served to focus the minds of the people upon God, reached multitudes with salvation, and rekindled spiritual fires in the hearts of believers. An example of a pastor who understood the times and applied the gospel to them was Richard Baxter.

When Baxter (1615-1691) assumed the pastorate in 1641 at Kidderminster, a town of three thousand people in northern England, the church needed revitalization. Shortly after his arrival, he began to conduct conferences and catechisms for fourteen families a week on his church field. He taught them the gospel, showing them how the message of Scripture impacted all of life. Through Bible classes for the people and preaching with a spiritual power that was not known before in the church, the Holy Spirit began to move within the church membership. As the crowds grew, five additions to the sanctuary had to be built. The crowds still overflowed the auditorium. Before he came spiritual matters were seldom mentioned in the marketplace; after the renewal began to ignite, one could hear people singing the songs of the faith as they walked along the streets. As the people rejoiced in the fellowship with God, multitudes of people were converted and some of the most immoral people of the town were saved.

In the midst of this revival, Baxter wrote several monumental works. In 1647, Baxter became critically ill and was bedridden for five months. While convalescing, he recorded his reflections on his "journey to the gates of Eternity." In 1649/1650, he published the classic called *The Saint's Everlasting Rest*. On December 4, 1655, he was scheduled to preach the inaugural message for the Association of pastors in the county where Kidderminster is located. Due to illness, he was unable to fulfill the commitment. However, he expanded the message for that occasion into a book that was published 1656 under the title *The Reformed Pastor*. This work is still considered one of the greatest works of practical advice for the pastor. In our day one may automatically think of Reformed theology by the title, but by "Reformed," Baxter meant that the preacher must serve with a spiritual vitality, or in the midst of awakening. In 1657, he

---

Richard Baxter's advice to pastors, from *The Reformed Pastor:*

--[Your people] will likely feel when you have been much with God: that which is most on your hearts, is like to be most in their ears.

--We must study as hard how to live well, as how to preach well.

--Brethren, if the saving of souls be your end, you will certainly intend it out of the pulpit as well as in it! . . . Oh that this were your daily study, how to use your wealth, your friends, and all you have for God, as well as your tongues!

--You are not like to see any general reformation, till you procure family reformation.

--The ministerial work must be carried on purely for God and the salvation of souls, not for any private ends of our own.

--Prayer must carry on our work as well as preaching: he preacheth not heartily to his people, that prayeth not earnestly for them.

--Oh, speak not one cold or careless word around so great a business as heaven or hell.

--O brethren, what a blow we may give to the kingdom of darkness, by the faithful and skillful managing of His work! If then, the saving of souls, of your neighbour's souls, many souls, from everlasting misery, be worth your labour, up and be doing!

--I would throw aside all the libraries in the world, rather than be guilty of the perdition of one soul.

---

published the classic entitled *The Call to the Unconverted.* Baxter led his church to a remarkable season of renewal and revitalization. Study his life to be encouraged.

A Book to Read for Vision

Recently several of our classes came together to hear from North American Mission Board leader Jeff Christopherson. Jeff talked about Kingdom ministry and offered some helpful insights into where we are today from his brand-new book *Kingdom Matrix*. I immediately bought the book on my Amazon Kindle. He offered an example from his own ministry context in Canada as a church planter that I found especially compelling. He spoke about gathering 60 unbelievers, almost all of them completely unchurched. He asked them this question: when they think of spirituality, what do they value?

They sat around tables, discussed it, and came up with three things:

1. God would be important every day to me, not just one day.

2. We would have community that would care for each other and look after our needs.

3. Our community would care for and take responsibility for the larger community.

I found this to be interesting. Jeff observed how this looks a lot like the latter verse of Acts 2 describing the early church. I lead a ministry at our church, Richland Creek Community Church, a young church plant of about 15 years now that has grown dramatically since its birth to close to 2000 in worship. I lead the ministry to young professionals or "young pros" as we call them. Our ministry is based on three core truths:

1. Knowing God through the gospel in such a way that all of life is changed, every day.

2. Community groups in homes, led by married couples with life experiences beyond the group (i.e. older as in Titus 2). These groups become as precious for many as their own families.

3. Care for those around us who do not know Christ, and care for our community as well. I even quote Hard Rock's saying "love all, serve all" at our website to remind our folks we are not just a bunch of church goers trying to act more religious, but we are Christ-followers who seek to be agents of redemption.

> Key to a revitalized church: Gospel + Community + Mission

I do not advocate a "seeker-driven" approach to ministry. But the reflections of the 60 folks Jeff mentioned does show us something we often miss in our evangelism today: every person was created in the imago of God. Every person. Lost people too. Sin has blinded their minds and corrupted their souls, but that does not mean they have no capacity whatsoever to see truth. Paul understood this in Acts 17 when he started with an idol and their limited belief in a creating deity to move them to see the gospel. This is why we can appreciate and value everything from art to sports whether they have an explicitly "Christian" focus or not: we can see the *imago dei* in the artists, musicians, athletes, and others.

Lost people do not know Christ. They have been blinded. They are dead in sin. But they are not totally incapable of seeing truth. Augustine in his *Confessions* talked about his journey to faith, and how God used other ideas that did not have the whole truth to push him over time to see the truth found only in Christ. We can take the spiritual hunger of unbelievers, who seek community, most of whom believe in God in some manner and would like to know more about Him, and we can guide them to Jesus.

By the way, of those 60 Jeff mentioned, over 50 ultimately came to Christ. He took their interest and their hunger and walked with them to Jesus. We can do that as well. And, truth is we want those same three things as well, don't we?

Take Action:

Does your church exhibit both numerically and from the perspective of people in your community a sense of health, vigor, and growth?

Does your passion for God permeate all your life? If you are a leader, does helping those you lead to become increasingly passionate and effective regarding the mission of God to bring Him glory and to fulfill the Great Commission consume you?

What price would you pay to see your church revitalized?

--Take a few minutes to think about the gospel. Stop

and reflect on the world around you. Do you see its beauty? Can you imagine one part of Creation that still brings awe? Do you see reminders of the Fall and its effects? Do you reflect daily on the Rescue of Christ? Do you yearn for the Restoration?

Chapter Two
INGESTION: From a Diet of Junk Food Spirituality to a Gospel Feast

"May the strength of God pilot us, may the wisdom of God instruct us, may the hand of God protect us, and may the Word of God direct us."

Saint Patrick

Imagine two scenarios:

A: You work at a factory where you are one of two thousand employees who do essentially the same job at the same kind of machine over three shifts week after week. You get paid well enough to get by, but you have no say in the company and are simply expected to do your job, nothing more.

B: You are part of a new startup company in which every employee's opinion matters. You are treated like a valuable member of a team and you find your ideas being considered and at times adopted. Your company has the potential of making significant changes that will affect people's lives in a positive way.

Some people would prefer the safe, mundane job described in scene A. But most would rather be a part of something like scene B. But there is also the fact that in each case people are being compensated and thus can take care of their families. In a local church, where people voluntarily attend, support, and live out their faith together and separately, the two scenarios would matter more would they not?

As I have traveled across the country and interacted with thousands of pastors I find the biggest frustration to be the apathy of so many members. But study the history of spiritual renewal and revival and you will see testimonies of the Bible coming alive in the lives of believers, families, and churches. Just as a body that feeds on a nutritionally weak diet will eventually suffer the effects of lethargy, a church fed on a malnourished spiritual diet will slide into apathy.

Years ago I taught at a university. One spring we saw a moving of the Spirit in the lives of some of our students. In some cases students confessed hidden sins from pornography to dishonesty. In this season two young ladies admitted their addiction to an eating disorder, one to anorexia and the other to bulimia. I was stunned, as each lady seemed otherwise to be a bright, beautiful, passionate follower of Jesus. But each had been convinced that they were grossly overweight and unacceptable, leading to starving themselves almost to death. At the same time, across our nation and in our churches we see more than ever who struggle with immense obesity.

We see the same in our churches. Some take one aspect of biblical truth and instead of seeing it through gospel lenses they give it inordinate attention, like an anorexic that becomes obsessed with weight loss. Some take the obvious biblical teaching on obeying God and His commands and focus on rules to the neglect of grace, leading to a Pharisaical legalism so common today. On the other hand, some take to an extreme the biblical teaching on grace and neglect obedience and become antinomian.

Others become fat, seriously fat Christians. Feasting on the junk food of the Christian subculture and the high carbs of church activity, they reek of religious jargon and deeds while neglecting the fit, healthy life of a surrendered disciple.

Like a human body starved for nutrition either by under-eating or overeating, many churches are filled with activities but manifest very little true spiritual life, and as a result bear little fruit. One can be so "active" at the church building that he can fool himself into thinking that simply being busy in church work automatically brings a fruitful and a faithful life. But this is not so. Read Matthew 23 and see Jesus' diatribe against the Pharisees who saw themselves as robust, healthy God-followers while actually being dead on the inside.

We all know people who looked perfectly fine until they suddenly died of a heart attack. We know people who seemed fit only to discover their body was riddled with cancer. We also read of the church of Ephesus in Revelation 2 that on the surface seemed healthy in effort and conviction, but they suffered from the most serious malady of all: they had abandoned their love for Christ.

It takes 3500 calories to make one pound. We typically need somewhere around 1500-2000 calories, give or take a lot depending on your size, fitness level, and other factors. If you eat a large order of French fries at Five Guys Hamburgers, you will eat almost 1500 calories. And, some really unhealthy calories! If you want to lose 3500 calories or the equivalent of a pound, you need to walk 20 miles slowly (or 10 miles rapidly), or you could swim for four hours. In other words, if you are overweight and want to lose weight, you need to get moving. *But the most important movement is to stop eating food that is bad for you.* The biggest myth of some (not all) of the fitness emphases of our times is that you can simply exercise your way to health. No, you have to eat your way there as well. Losing weight is really not that hard: just eat less food, and especially the food that is really bad for you. Okay, easier said than done. For me, the greatest aid in losing weight was a calorie counting app on my phone. When I consistently log in what I eat daily, my weight stays constant. Believers individually and churches in general need such an aid, some way to help us stay focused on a healthy spiritual diet. That includes learning how to eat better. In the same way, we learn to grow spiritually by feasting less on the toxic food of the world and the junk food of Christian religious activity or tangents, and more on prayerful study of God's Word.

Give Them Meat

I find it fascinating that over the last several years numerous large, rapidly growing churches across the U.S. have been marked by pastors who preach sermons verse by verse, focusing on Jesus and His gospel, and often their sermons last an hour or more: people like David Platt, J.D. Greear, Matt Chandler, Darrin Patrick, to name only a few. My own pastor teaches the word verse by verse, book by book, and our church has grown rapidly in her 15 years of existence. And, Johnny Hunt and others have seen such growth for years doing the same thing. It seems there is a correlation between churches eating a healthy diet of Scriptural truth and subsequent spiritual vitality. Studies show that the churches that reach young adults in significant numbers today do so in large part because they offer depth and are not afraid to deal with hard questions. Our God is a consistent God, so it is not surprising that the same principles that apply physically for a human body also apply spiritually to nurturing our spirits and intellectually to growing our minds in a God-ward direction.

A few years ago the largest study on youth and religion ever conducted in the United States concluded that the diet we are feeding young people makes them spiritually fat, dull, and lethargic. Many are going to other spiritual avenues to find what they perceive as healthier fare. Moralistic Therapeutic Deism is the name for the current form of junk food Christianity. In a scathing critique of current youth ministry based on the study, Kendra Dean observes:

> After two and a half centuries of shacking up with "the American dream," churches have perfected a dicey codependence between consumer-driven therapeutic individualism and religious pragmatism. These theological proxies gnaw, termite-like, at our identity as the Body of Christ, eroding our ability to recognize that Jesus' life of self-giving love directly challenges the American gospel of self-fulfillment and self-actualization. . . . [That] American young people

are unwittingly being formed into an imposter faith that poses as Christianity, but that in fact lacks the holy desire and missional clarity necessary for Christian discipleship—will not be solved by youth ministry or by persuading teenagers to commit more wholeheartedly to lackluster faith. . . . At issue is our ability, and our willingness, to remember our identity as the Body of Christ, and to heed Christ's call to love him and love others as his representatives in the world.[v]

Dean goes on to note that the church has taught youth too well an emaciated diet that has not been effective:

The problem does not seem to be that churches are teaching young people badly, but that we are doing an exceedingly good job of teaching youth what we really believe: namely, that Christianity is not a big deal, that God requires little, and the church is a helpful social institution filled with nice people focused primarily on "folks like us"—which, of course, begs the question of whether we are really the church at all.[vi]

Just last week I had lunch with a pastor who had become acquainted with the term Moralistic Therapeutic Deism and confessed his participation in teaching this without even realizing it. He was broken over the realization that in the name of teaching the Word he had in fact been feeding his flock a knock-off version of biblical teaching that has some truth but misses the heart of our faith. What is this diet?

It is *Moralistic* because the focus is on changing morality, or behavior modification. We have taken a *result* of the change made by the gospel (moral change) and made it synonymous *with* the gospel. In this approach, Jesus died and rose again to give us life, most especially seen in heaven after we die. In the meantime, our goal in life is to get better, especially in our moral lives. I had just this talk with a student yesterday, who upon reflecting on his upbringing in church realized his goal as a Christian had been far more about becoming increasingly moral and little about sacrificing one's life for the mission of God. Make no mistake: when we meet Jesus it changes our morality. The Bible has a lot of teaching on this. But it comes as the result of the gospel and should never be confused with the work of grace in Christ, for to do so makes us pretty good Pharisees but pretty lame missionaries.

This teaching is *Therapeutic* because it implies the primary goal is to make us feel better, to help us to cope with life. This eventually makes us the center of the Story of the Bible in the place of Jesus. When we teach about David and Goliath we make ourselves synonymous with David, and we become the hero of the story. No, David points us to God as Rescuer, and ultimately to Christ. It is *Deistic* because God becomes less and less intimate and involved in our lives, so we live practically as if He is not involved except when we are at church or involved in an explicitly spiritual endeavor.

A steady diet of this over years leads people like David Kinnaman to research young adults and write a book called *You Lost Me,* chronicling why so many young adults today do not want to feed on what the church is serving. But the good news is more and more recognize this issue and are confronting it. In the Great Awakenings churches were revitalized as they confronted the idols of their time with the gospel and returned to Christ and the Word. By the way, in these great revivals the primary subject preached was not how to have revival; they preached the gospel!

To counter the junk food religious diet of MTD, a revitalized church feeds on the Word and thirsts for prayer. The saints we read about in Acts 4 turned to God in prayer and focused on God as active, involved, and available to His children. There was no spiritual compartmentalization for them, as their prayer and passion led to sacrifice of material goods and even to the point of some sacrificing their very lives (4:29-33). A revitalized church has a holistic view of God and their relationship to Him. Prayer marks such a people, because they have a conviction that although God is great and sovereign and far beyond them, He is also near to them and involved both in their churches and their lives. You will never get to the place in ministry where you are successful, gifted, wise, or intelligent enough to lead without a deep, earnest life of prayer.

As a young pastor I came to serve a church that had nine in Sunday school our first Sunday. We were pitiful and then we had a relapse! I was ignorance on fire, and did not really have a clue how to revitalize this church. So we began to pray. We turned Wednesday night Prayer meeting into a real time of prayer. I began to set aside time weekly to pray over every name of every person who was a member or potential member. Then, we held an all night prayer meeting, crying out to God. The next week we saw more come to Christ than the church had seen in almost a decade. I believe in the power of prayer. S.D. Gordon said it well: "You can do more than pray after you have prayed, but you cannot do more than pray until you have prayed."

Give Them Fresh Food

One of the practical lessons I tell my students about dieting: when you go to the grocery store, spend most of your money on the foods found at the outside of the store. This is the stuff God made: fresh produce, milk, eggs, cheese, meats, things that have been far less processed and stripped of essential, natural nutrients.

Give people fresh, real teaching from the Word more than prepackaged programming. Repackaged sermons from podcasts will never feed people like a fresh word from God spoken to your life. Simply getting more teaching, more church activity, and more of the same only seems to make people busier, not healthier, while churches grow more lethargic. We must change the diet people are feasting on. In his book *The Four Hour Body* Tim Ferris describes friends from Brazil who have petite Argentine girlfriends who gained 10-20 pounds rapidly when they came to the U.S. Why? The much larger portion sizes and the rapidity with which we eat. Could it be that we have stagnant churches in part because we are so involved in activities that keep us busy and often hurried in our church buildings while doing little to strengthen our faith or to push us to develop, so that we set aside the message and the mission of God for a religious, moralistic busyness?

Take your people out to dine on the gospel: mission trips can be a phenomenal way to activate the gospel's reality in a people. Many times a fresh vision has come to a local church after members witnessed the power of the gospel at work on a mission trip to the nations. Do not simply teach the gospel, but also take your people out to see the gospel at work!

A Model of a Feasting Church – Frelinghuysen

Study the lives of those in history and today who have led revitalizing efforts in churches and you will see people deeply in love with Jesus and sincerely devoted to him. Robert Murray McCheyne, who saw revival in his church as a young man in Scotland, said this: "God does not bless great talent, He blesses great likeness to Jesus." The issue is less your ability and more your proximity to Christ. Cultivate your own walk with Christ. Feast on His Word. Resolve to be known for your prayer life over your social life.

In an excellent blog post on revitalization pastor J.D. Greear of the Summit Church in Raleigh-Durham – a remarkable story of revitalization – offers advice on leading a church to change. His first lesson: "inward transformation drives external change." He observes that the faithful teaching on the gospel will eventually bring about change, but he also warns that at times change will not come as quickly as we wish because the people must first be taught to move from a moralistic or other view of Christianity to a biblical one, and this can only come through knowing the Word.[vii]

An example of the revitalizing effects of a healthy biblical diet comes from the early days of the First Great Awakening and the ministry of pastor Theodore Jackobus

Frelinghuysen (1691-1747). A German born in a time of Pietistic renewal in his homeland, Frelinghuysen came to the colonies in 1720, filled with missionary zeal to serve as pastor of four small, part-time churches in the Raritan Valley of New Jersey.

While in New Jersey he experienced the first sparks of the awakening's fire in the year 1726. The great evangelist George Whitefield in 1739 called Frelinghuysen "a worthy old soldier of Jesus Christ, . . . and the beginner of the great work which I trust the Lord is carrying on in these parts."[viii]

Frelinghuysen came to the New World with a burning passion for God sparked by a spiritual movement there. He soon learned he had come to serve small, established churches marked by worldliness and apathy, not spiritual vitality. He commented on the spiritual laxity in the churches he served: "... while horse-racing, gambling, dissipation, and rudeness of various kinds were common, the [church] was attended at convenience, and religion consisted of the mere formal pursuit of the routine of duty."[ix] Does that sound familiar? The members considered the practice of the Lord's Supper (which they observed weekly), Baptism, and church attendance to be the sum total of their religious duty. The young pastor began to seek the face of God on behalf of his flock.

Frelinghuysen determined to see fresh vigor for Christ through a simple approach: a regular diet of gospel preaching, church discipline (especially related to observing the Lord's Supper), and zealous visitation. His preaching on the necessity of conversion, particularly when aimed at church members, brought both a spirit of revival with many converts resulting and controversy among some members and other ministers. Many members welcomed his leadership, though some fought unsuccessfully to oust him as pastor. NOTE: if you seek to revitalize a stagnant church, you must be a shepherd who loves his sheep, even when the sheep stink. But you must also understand that there will be wolves, and one way to determine the shepherd's love for his sheep is how he responds when wolves appear.

Many church members were converted under his

ministry, a mark of deep revival. In 1725 a group published seventeen charges charging him with doctrinal error and improper practices. Frelinghuysen responded with these words: "I care not what carnal, ignorant men say behind my back. They are greatly deceived if they imagine they will thus put me to shame, for I would rather die a thousand deaths than not preach the truth."[x]

Despite opposition, renewal flourished. It reached its climax in 1726 and was especially powerful among the youth of the four churches served by Frelinghuysen. We must remember that seasons of revitalization are like a fire: some draw near to it for its warmth, while others fear the heat it can bring. The fire of the Spirit exposes all sin, with a result that one will come to God's light for purging and refining, or run from God to hide in the darkness.

Frelinghuysen focused on the necessity of conversion, which came through justification by faith alone. This hearty teaching fed the people and grew them.

We live in a day of fad diets, pills, and quick fixes. Revitalizing a church is less like steering a jet ski and more like maneuvering an aircraft carrier: it takes a lot of time and a lot of space. I have seen men who were grossly overweight lose a lot of weight only to gain it back. But I have also seen men lose the weight, keep it off, and become like a new person. You do not accomplish this change on a whim or with a fad. A church will not change overnight. It takes time and a steady diet of prayer and the Word to change her. The early apostles understood the diet a church needs, for in Acts 6 they recognized they needed others to help them so they could give themselves to the ministry of the Word and prayer. If you are a pastor, you have no calling more vital than to lead your people by teaching the Word faithfully and building a praying congregation.

I have a friend who came to a stagnant church of about 200 or so in attendance. He began to develop prayer groups and made a ministry of prayer a fundamental feature of that body, while faithfully teaching the Word. Over the next two decades the church, while in a terrible location and with plenty of excuses not to grow, became a huge force for the gospel and a congregation of over 4000 weekly. Read the Acts again and see how much prayer marked the early church. Note how the early believers in Acts 2:42 gave themselves first to doctrine, and to prayer.

A Helpful Book

My friend and former student J.D. Greear wrote a wonderful book called *Gospel: Recovering the Power That Made Christianity Revolutionary.* He unpacks the glory of the gospel in terms that make sense to the churchgoer and the novice believer. A companion study can be used to help your church understand the revolutionary nature of the gospel.

Take Action:

This very weekend I am in two very different churches (one a Chinese Nondenominational Church in an urban setting, the other a large Baptist Church in a large town) where I will be teaching The Story (go to www.viewthestory.com or www.thestorytraining.com). I highly encourage you to consider this as a tool to help believers understand several keys truths: 1) the Bible is one great Story focusing on a redeeming God; 2) Jesus is the only hope of the world; 3) the good news in Christ is both for the unbeliever for salvation and the believer for sanctification; 4) telling this Story in everyday conversations will grow a gospel awareness and hunger in your community.

Chapter Three
TRACTION: Exercise Your Faith by Living the Mission Daily

"There is nothing wrong with change, if it is in the right direction." Winston Churchill

"Do not underestimate the power of momentum." J.D. Greear

If you have gotten to this page and are ready to see your church change, or are motivated to continue on the path of change you started, or even if you feel overwhelmed and are still unsure of how to get started, we now become really practical. Whether talking about your physical body or the body of Christ, here is how change happens.

When it is time to change in a way that costs us, three things musthappen. ***First, we need to understand rationally the need to change.*** Our minds must see the need to change. Information does not always lead to transformation. Smokers who know they need to quit normally do not, for instance. Just because a believer knows he or she should witness simply will not automatically lead to an evangelistic lifestyle. But we do need such information to help bring about change. *When the pain of the status quo is less than the cost of change, you are ready to get after it.* When a burden for reaching the lost in your community and the nations, and when seeing believers live for Jesus with a passion, when these things consume you, you are ready for change. Change will cost you, make no mistake about it.

You do not have to know you personally to know two

things about you. First, to this point your life has not turned out exactly like you thought it would. This is no doubt true of your church as well. Second, inside you there is a burden, a fire, and a hunger for your life to matter for something more than survival. You want your life to count and you want your church to matter for the Kingdom of God. As Jeff Christopherson says in his helpful book *Kingdom Matrix*, we are either advancing the dominion of darkness or advancing the Kingdom of God! Being convinced that nothing matters more than the glory of God and spreading His fame must be true of your life and some in leadership if you will see revitalization realized. Are you sick and tired of being sick and tired? This is true whether we are talking about your physical life, your devotional life, or your church's life. Once you realize you are ready to pay whatever price to see God move in your church afresh, you are ready to move.

Demographic information on such issues as your church's history, the community around you – the percentage of unchurched, the numbers of young families, etc. – can help to see reality. Mission boards and local church associations and networks can help with this.

Second, to change when change is hard, we need a *compelling vision*. The vision must be big, requiring serious commitment. The Harvard School of Business calls this a BHAG, or Big Hairy Audacious Goal. Look at the calendar. Add five years to today's date. Where would you like your church to be then? How about in 20 years? Those who believe God is able to bring about remarkable things lead revitalized churches. But make no mistake: God's level of blessing typically rises to the level of our expectation. Look at pastors in history who led revitalizing churches, from McCheyne to Spurgeon, from Baxter to Criswell. These men all had a compelling vision to do something for which only God could be given credit.

We are talking here about lifestyle change, a new vision, not a quick fix. *Again, when the pain of change is less than the pain of the status quo, we will change.* When I hit age 50, I began to get a vision for serving Christ well into my

70s and beyond, and having more energy now. As a result today I am about 40 pounds lighter and in much better overall health (according to my doctor) than I have been in years. It took time, but it would never have happened without a compelling vision. In the wonderful video introducing his book *Church Planter*, Darrin Patrick mentions a man who had a greater vision for a certain church than the pastor himself had. Patrick went on to say he did not want anyone to have a greater vision that he had for the church God called him to serve!

See the Darrin Patrick video at
http://www.youtube.com/watch?v=XnN2PrIQijw

But I would argue we still need one thing more. Yes, we need to see that we must change. We also need a vision big enough to require genuine commitment, but one that offers hope. But we are all human, and discouragement is one of the major factors in men leaving ministry. How do we have a compelling vision when we see the need to change, and yet not lose heart?

Third, we need *short term wins to keep the vision alive.* In the Acts we read about Peter's discovery that the gospel was for Gentiles. Peter knew intellectually that the gospel was for all. Yet when it came to Gentiles, he needed a compelling vision to see clearly they could receive the same gospel the Jews received. He got it, a real vision in fact, as we read in Acts 10. Rationally, he knew the Great Commission was for all. Then he received a compelling vision that he should not consider unclean those God considered clean. But then, he had a short term "win" in the form of Cornelius, a Gentile Peter led to Christ.

In his article on revitalization, J.D. Greear reminds us that momentum matters greatly. He recommends focusing on developing those who seek change than on engaging those who are against it. "Instead of spending a lot of time putting out fires, you might want to start one of your own," he writes.[xi]

I served as a pastor of a small church while in seminary. The church had declined for years and had seen no new converts baptized in five years, and only three people baptized in the previous eight years. The baptistery held the Christmas decorations, serving as a closet. I came to the church and was ignorance on fire. I made a lot of young pastor's mistakes. But I did believe in prayer and I believed God had called this church to reach her community. The church members knew we had to grow to survive.

Both I -- and key leaders -- knew we needed to change, to grow. We did have a vision for impact in the community and to grow in spirit and truth. But we desperately needed some short-term wins. We scheduled an evangelistic meeting. We prayed, all night one night in fact, and we did everything we knew to do to spread the word from radio ads to door-to-door invitations. I told the folks the Sunday before the evangelistic meeting that I had asked God for ten people to be saved and baptized. Then I thought, "That was really stupid—they have not seen ten people reached in ten years!" But I truly believed we needed to trust God for something of eternal significance. We needed a short term win, a glimpse of God at work in our midst. That Wednesday night a family who had visited told us their daughter had trusted Christ and would join Sunday morning. I think the Lord knew this young preacher needed a short term win!

That following Sunday-Wednesday our little church had our meeting, and by the following Sunday I had baptized ten new believers. I remember to this day the anxiety, the doubt that filled my heart before God moved. I would not trade that sense of hope and yet fear, and the joy of seeing God move in our midst, for anything!

There have been other times since then that I have followed a similar plan, whether in my personal life or in a larger ministry. In my current role as leader of our young professionals ministry at our church we have seen God do similar work. Sometimes we are so afraid of being presumptuous in our faith we end up believing God for little to nothing. What is happening in your life and ministry just now that can only be explained by the fact that Jesus rose from the dead?

A simple plan of discipleship with less activity can actually produce more growth than a lot of busyness. As a young man I attended church faithfully. A typical week looked something like this:

--Sunday morning: Sunday school and worship (2 times of learning) ---Sunday evening: Discipleship training and worship (2 times of learning)

--Wednesday night: Another time of learning.

This means I learned five different lessons weekly. All were disconnected, unique lessons. I remember next to nothing from all those years. No doubt the cumulative effect of all these times of learning helped to form me; but I submit that nailing down a clear biblical focus with less varied lessons over time will do more to make disciples than a hodgepodge of subjects ever will. As a teacher I would rather folks learn one significant truth of Scripture a week and make application to their lives than learn several things, none of which make it to application.

Recent research in fitness demonstrates how High Intensity Training (workouts done less frequently but to muscle failure) has a far more powerful impact on the human body than moderate exercise. I believe God set up the world to be coherent and consistent whether we are talking about spiritual or physical change. I would argue that deep, intense biblical teaching on less topics week after week will do more to make disciples than a lot of disconnected teaching, just like High Intensity Training affects one's body more than disconnected exercising at a less intense level.

When you teach deep, rich, consistent truth to your people, and as people begin to respond, you develop something a church must have to experience revitalization: *momentum*. When traction comes and momentum begins to grow, change can happen.

Shift to Missional Evangelism

On a practical level, this means increasingly helping

those we lead to live their faith as passionately in the community as they sing about it in a church service. This will lead to a shift from what I call "presentational" evangelism to missional evangelism. In a missional witness conversations matter more than presentations. When a missionary moves overseas to plant her life in a different culture, every conversation matters, whether the gospel is shared explicitly or not. We now live in one of the largest mission fields on earth, so the same applies here. In fact, the fastest growing religious group in the United States is the "Nones," or those with no religious affiliation.[xii] These are not all atheists, but they increasingly, especially among younger Americans, see little need for a perceived institutional religion like a church. What we may actually be seeing is a growing divide between those who passionately follow Christ and those who have no affiliation, with the nominal middle shrinking in an accelerating pace. In a new and helpful book called *Everyday Church* Tim Chester and Steve Timmis offer a helpful perspective on churches in the West today:

> Much of the decline in the church in the West has been the falling off of nominal Christians. As a result, what remains may be healthier. We now have the opportunity to become communities focused on Jesus and his mission. The number of true Christians may not be falling so steeply – if at all. But what is fast disappearing is the opportunity to reach notionally religious people through church activities.[xiii]

If they are right, and I believe they are to a large extent, what we are seeing is a decline of institutional believers and attenders who are tied more to the local church and its traditions than to Christ and His mission. For those who know Christ and who remain, these offer the greatest hope for a revitalized church. If we can help these Christ followers to learn to see the world as missionaries do and respond as missionaries to those they know, we will help believers to grow in their witness. In an earlier book the same authors argued that this is the need of the hour: "ordinary people doing ordinary things with gospel intentionality."[xiv] It also means we focus our conversations on the worldview of those around us. It means helping people see how their personal story relates to God's greater Story seen in Scripture.

The Message of God is unchanging, but teaching that message involves relating it in a given culture in comprehensible ways. We have to see the gospel in its greatness and how it affects all of our lives. And we have to see people around us with new eyes as well.

When a person begins to exercise anew he must give attention to three areas: flexibility, muscle strength, and cardiovascular training. Ignoring one of these over time will come back to bite you. Similarly, our witness involves three community, worship, and mission. The more real our community is, the more authentic our worship, and the more focused we are on the mission, the better.

Practically speaking, this means we see our witness less as a presentation we seek to convince people to hear and respond, and more a conversation in which we begin in their worldview to show them the truth of the gospel.

The Bible teaches every person was created in the image of God. Even though the Fall has brought devastation to our world, and every person is now sinful and in need of a Savior, God also created them in His image. This is why we can admire a painting in a museum or a song on the radio, regardless of whether either was crafted by a Christian. We can see the glory of God in many places, and we can show this as a means to help people see God made us for so much more. God made us to worship, and the unique ways people – compared to anything else in the universe – design, build, craft, and display useful, beautiful, and helpful things in some way reflect His glory.

Presentational evangelism shows an unbeliever the gospel in our worldview and asks them to adopt that. Presentational evangelism was very effective in a cultural context where a generally common worldview was in place. It still is effective in areas where a general consensus exists in terms of worldview, like more rural communities in the South. News flash: that consensus no longer exists in our nation as a whole, and in particular in cities. Missional evangelism, however, starts in the worldview of the unbeliever, shows them truth they already affirm, and then moves from that truth to show the gospel, as Paul did in Lystra in Acts 14 and in Athens in Acts 17. Just this week I used movies and plot lines to show a server in Waffle House the gospel. She already believed movies have a storyline that often value a rescue, and she definitely loves movies with a happy ending and wants one for her. So I went from that to show her the biblical plot line and it made perfect sense to her. I have led more people to Christ in the last three years starting in their worldview like this than I have trying to get them to begin by agreeing with mine. Jesus began in the world of the fishermen Peter and John, the Samaritan woman, the Rich Young Ruler, and Zaccheus, to name only a few examples in the Gospels.

Note: missional evangelism is more conversational but no less intentional. In missional evangelism we see ways an unbeliever a) reflects the image of God in creative, helpful, or useful ways, and b) shows him truth that is God's truth, as Paul did in Acts 17. For instance, I led a young lady to Christ by talking with her about how beautiful the world is, and how everything around us has such harmony. She totally agreed. I then observed how something has gone wrong, and how people struggle with everything from natural disasters and disease to personal choices and circumstances. She agreed and offered more than a few examples. Then, I showed her how Jesus came not to get her to church services or to make her toe the line of a moral code, but He came to rescue people, including her, from the brokenness in the world caused by sin. She totally saw this and followed Christ. I have seen this repeated many times.

This also means we must do more than simply provide a place for people to come to in large numbers on Sundays, and more than a place that provides programs for general growth. We must invade our communities with a demonstration of Christ as well as a verbal communication of His truth.

Another feature of missional evangelism arises from

its ability to demonstrate the gospel's change while also announcing the gospel's message. In the books of Acts we read how the early church put the gospel on display in a variety of ways:

--They spoke it boldly (Acts 2:10-11; 4:13, 29-31)

--They cared for physical needs (Acts 2:44-45)

--They worshiped God unashamedly (Acts 2:47)

--They touched people in miraculous ways (Acts 2:43)

--They stood in the face of persecution (Acts 4:20)

--They were continuously filled with praise (Acts 2:47)

--They were unambiguous in their zeal for their mission (Acts 4:8-13)

--They loved the marginalized in their culture (Acts 3)

What are ways you could display the gospel in your area? What are ways you can consistently show what you believe even while you share it?

Pietistic Revitalization

After the radical changes that came about from the Protestant Reformation, much of Germany and Europe became populated with new churches. Lutheranism thrived, as did other post-Reformation groups. But as is the case throughout history, Lutheran churches became established, institutionalized, and many fossilized over time. A movement called Pietism exploded in revitalizing power with the publication in 1675 of Philip Spener's *Pia Desideria*, or "Pious Desires."[xv] This classic in Christian spirituality was a manual of reform for Lutheran churches. Under the influence of Spener, Jean DeLabadie, August H. Francke, Moravian leader Count Nicolaus Von Zinzendorf, and others, Pietism made a notable impact upon Lutheran, Reformed, and other churches. Pietism emphasized individual devotion to God, a conversion experience, serious Bible study, and hymn singing. As noted earlier, the Pietists influenced leaders of later movements such as Frelinghuysen.

Pietists typically saw themselves as a second phase of the Protestant Reformation. Luther and others brought renewal to matters of orthodoxy (historic Christian belief); the concern of the Pietists was that there be a concomitant orthopraxy (historic Christian practice). Vance Havner once said you can be a straight as a gun barrel and just as empty. In other words, you can have doctrinal purity and be dead as a hammer. "Justification by faith alone" was the Reformation cry; "you must be born again" served as the clarion call of Pietism.

Lewis Drummond, who called *Pia Desideria* the "manifesto of the movement," listed eight characteristics of this "new Lutheran bolt of lightning:"[xvi] the new birth, religious enthusiasm, felicity or a joyous feeling of communion with Christ, sanctification, biblicism, theological education, missionary-evangelism, and social concern.[xvii] I think you can see how these emphases would help bring dead churches alive again.

Spener considered himself an orthodox Lutheran, citing Luther extensively in *Pia Desideria*. He and other Lutheran Pietists insisted that they were not innovators, but were bringing the people back to the goals of Luther. While at Strasbourg, he was influenced by his professor John Schmid; the works of Martin Luther; Johann Arndt; the English Puritan Richard Baxter; and Theophilus Groszgebauer, the author of *A Watchman's Cry from Devastated Zion*. During 1660-1661, he journeyed to Basel and Geneva. Spener came under the influence of Jean de Labadie, a fiery preacher of repentance, at Geneva. Our passion for revitalization will begin and spread in no small part based both on the people who influence us and the books we read.

Upon his return to Germany in 1661, Spener began a growing ministry of the Word of God. Pastorates in Frankfurt, Dresden, and Berlin helped him to become the most renowned minister in his day. He was concerned with the growing worldliness in the Lutheran church and its overemphasis on the sacraments. In 1666, Spener began the *Collogia Pietatis*, or "exercises of piety," a gathering of believers to study Scripture and the practice of Christianity. The meetings touched a hunger in the spiritual life of area believers. Interest in these meetings caused them to multiply across the city. Spener was called "A burning and shining light in his generation," an "instrument of blessing to nations, and a father to many thousands."[xviii] In *Pia Desideria* Spener offered specific guidelines for renewing the Lutheran church:

1. A greater commitment to spread the Word of God.

2. A renewed emphasis on the Lutheran view of the priesthood of all believers.

3. A greater focus given to the development of individual spiritual life.

4. Truth should not be established through disputes but through repentance and a holy life.

5. Candidates for the ministry should be genuine Christians, who have had spiritual training. Spener suggested Tauler's *Theological_Germanica*, which Luther greatly esteemed, Arndt's *True Christianity*, and Thomas a Kempis's *Imitation of Christ* as foundational study.

6. Sermons should not demonstrate the preacher's erudition, but attempt to edify.

Spener's fame grew to the point that he became chief court preacher in Saxony in 1686. He also faced opposition at every turn from a number of clergymen. Be careful of being envious of pastors whose churches grow; jealousy can kill your ministry. In 1690, he moved to Berlin. For fifteen years, Spener promoted Pietism in Berlin and surrounding areas. Through his preaching, the citizens of Berlin were constantly confronted with the spiritual demands of God upon their lives. By the time of his death on February 5, 1705, Pietism was entrenched as the catalyst for the great Pietistic Revivals of the eighteenth century. From this came a missionary movement that touched the world.

A Helpful Book: Comeback Churches

Books on revitalization number far less than books on church planting it seems, but one of the best on the former is the book by my friends Ed Stetzer and Mike Dodson,

Comeback Churches. This book examines many churches who have experienced revitalization.

Take Action:

What small steps could you take from this chapter? Remember a church is an aircraft carrier not a jet ski. Time, simple changes, and much prayer all matter.

What could you do in your specific spheres of influence to help develop traction for the gospel? How could you help other leaders do the same?

Chapter Four
ALIGNMENT: Marks of Gospel Focus

"Never lose heart in the power of the gospel. Do not believe that there exists any man, much less any race of men, for whom the gospel is not fitted." Spurgeon

Several years ago I sat next to a businessman on a plane. As I began to speak to him about Jesus, he told me with a smile of his love for Him. The next few minutes of conversation astounded me. This layman told me about his love for Jesus, and His church, and succinctly described the mission of his church. He told me of his teenaged daughter with whom he was going over seas soon on a mission trip. This man loved Jesus and was excited about his church. The church was Johnson Ferry Baptist Church, a large, vibrant church in the Atlanta area whose pastor Bryant Wright became president of the Southern Baptist Convention a few years later.

Perhaps this layman was unique in his church. Maybe he was the only man out of thousands there who could so clearly and passionately articulate his joy in Christ and devotion to his church. But I suspect there are many like him there.

If a typical, active member of your church had a

random conversation with a stranger, could they articulate with joy their love for Christ and their local church? Could they describe in a few sentences the mission of that church and their part in it?

At the beginning I mentioned my Spinal Stenosis. With Spinal Stenosis the discs in the lower back, though moist and spongy in early years, become more dry and stiff with age. The result, without being too technical, is the pinching of spinal nerves because of the spine's narrowing. The body still functions, but the effect over time is an increasing limitation of activity and eventually a desire to do little of anything except be a couch potato because of pain.

Too many churches today are in numerical decline or at best plateaued. Further, too many make little to no practical impact in the communities where they live. Question: If your church suddenly vanished from the community, who would notice?

The treatment for Spinal Stenosis varies based on the depth of the condition. For me, it is hoped that physical therapy will take care of it. This takes time as the nervous system overcomes trauma at a much slower rate than the muscular system. If this does not work, an epidural shot in the lower back should help. Eventually (hopefully never in my case), surgery may be required.

When one part of our body is significantly out of sync it affects everything. Getting adjustments to help the body function properly makes life altogether better. In the same way, a church lined up with the purposes of God finds living the mission to be a much more natural thing.

A Model of a Realigned, Revitalized, and Revived Church

One of the realities of church life is that all churches at times need a reassessment and often realignment. In this fallen and broken world we tend to drift from God not toward Him. And when churches do realign, revival often comes as a result. This happened in the ministry of Jonathan Edwards in the 1700s. The young pastor came to serve as pastor in Northampton, Massachusetts. The church had seen seasons of growth and renewal, but had moved into a state of stagnation. Soon the church and the region would be ignited in revival, and would eventually be a key part of the First Great Awakening, one of the most remarkable revivals in history. Edwards' first record of revival, the *Narrative,* chronicled the Valley Revival of 1734-35. Edwards was only thirty-one at the time. The Valley Revival spread from Northampton up and down the Connecticut River valley.

Revival brings revitalization at an escalated speed. Edwards observed several factors contributing to the revival's origin. Concerned about the dullness of the people toward the faith, Edwards called his people to honor the day of the Lord. This caused some to grow concerned over their laxity. This concern increased following the conversion of several families in the nearby town of Pascommuck.

Edwards also encouraged youth to form small groups for prayer and discussion, which they did. Soon many adults joined in as well. Edwards repeatedly commented on the preeminent role young people had in this and subsequent revivals. Do not underestimate the role youth can play in church revitalization. The death of two young people in separate incidents added to the growing seriousness of the people. Revival erupted when Edwards preached a series of messages on justification by faith. Edwards himself was amazed at what he termed the "surprising works of God." He wrote that for some time in Northampton the topic of discussion for everyone centered on spiritual matters. Many persons came to Christ as a result of the supernatural activity of God – about half the town in fact. A frivolous young woman's dramatic conversion was the first of many. Over three hundred professed faith in Christ in only six months.

What led to the work of God bringing revitalization to Edwards' church?

--Calling the people to honor the Lord.

--Challenging the youth to seek the Lord (implied in this was his belief that God could and would use them).

--He preached the gospel, not "how to get revival."

--They witnessed some powerful conversions.

--They knew it could not be explained in human terms.

By the spring of 1735 the church was crowded to capacity each week. Often the entire congregation was moved to tears due in some cases to joy, in others to sorrow for sin. In the months of March and April, nearly thirty were added to the church in addition to the spirit of revival among the believers. People came from other areas to see the amazing work. Many of them were awakened and spread the revival elsewhere. Edwards recorded that no less than twenty-seven towns ultimately experienced revival. Soon Edwards' church counted over six hundred members, encompassing virtually the entire adult population of the town.

The *Narrative* had a powerful effect on both the contemporary scene and over the century following. It was immediately published and sent to England. It had a profound effect on a young John Wesley. Wesley read the account in 1738, writing in his journal that this movement was surely from the Lord. As a result he "was led to desire earnestly that England might not lay behind America in that path of grace."[xix] Not long after God use Wesley and others to see a great spiritual movement there. In addition, evangelist George Whitefield read the work while in Georgia in 1738.

Due to his growing reputation as a preacher following the Valley Revival, Edwards occasionally traveled to other churches to speak and was used by God to help other churches experience renewal and revitalization. Edwards would no doubt seem out of sorts as a preacher today. But he fit the culture and times in which he lived, and we should as well. He was an exegetical preacher in the Puritan tradition. He typically stood in the pulpit with his manuscript in one hand and a candle in the other. Early in his ministry sermon manuscripts were read; after Whitefield visited Northampton, Edwards began using outlines instead. Winslow offers a telling glimpse of a Sunday in Northampton during Edwards' day:

It was on Sunday morning at the ringing of the

> meetinghouse bell that Northampton had its best
> chance to know 'Mr. Edwards,' as he mounted his high
> pulpit and in a quiet voice, without movement or
> gesture, laid down his doctrine. . . . the piercing eyes
> went everywhere, the thin tones reached the dim
> corners of the gallery. Every word was distinctively
> spoken. . . . This delicate-looking young man had
> something to say, and strangely enough his fragility
> seemed to increase his power.[xx]

You do not have to copy whoever is the most popular
or effective preacher of our time to lead a church to
revitalize. But you do need to lead people to see the glorious
gospel and the amazing God we serve. On July 8, 1741, he
preached his most renowned sermon, "Sinners in the Hands
of an Angry God," which spurred profound brokenness and
repentance in the church. His sermons were not all in the
imprecatory style of "Sinners." In fact, revival came to
Northampton in 1740 in the midst of a series on the love of
Christ from I Corinthians 13. Still, the impact of "Sinners"
should not be overlooked. The sermon featured incredible
imagery employed by Edwards. Based on the text Deut.
32:35, "Their foot shall slide in due time," Edwards' thesis
was "There is nothing that keeps wicked men at any one
moment out of hell, but the mere pleasure of God." His
imagery is almost visceral in its effect:

> The God that holds you over the pit of hell,
> much as one holds a spider or some loathsome insect
> over the fire, abhors you and is dreadfully
> provoked. His wrath toward you burns like fire; he
> looks upon you as worthy of nothing else but to be
> cast into the fire....it is nothing but His hand that
> holds you from falling into the fire every moment.[xxi]

He concluded the message with an appeal to flee the
wrath to come and follow Christ. What happened as he
delivered the message? "The effect of the sermon was as if
some supernatural apparition had frightened the people
beyond control," Allen observed. "They were convulsed in

tears of agony and distress. Amid their tears and outcries the preacher pauses, bidding them to be quiet in order that he may be heard."xxii

In January of 1742, he preached for several weeks in Leicester, where again awakening erupted. While on that tour he asked a Rev. Buell to preach in Northampton. As a result, "almost the whole town seemed to be in a great and continual commotion, day and night, and there was indeed a very great revival of religion . . . . When I came home, I found the town in very extraordinary circumstances, such as, in some respects, I never saw it before."xxiii In May, Edwards led the people to affirm a covenant before God, followed by a day of fasting.

A Biblical Realignment: Edwards' *Distinguishing Marks*

I mention Edwards not only because he saw a movement of revitalization and revival in his church, but also because his writings give guidance for others. He wrote a treatise describing the marks of a genuine work of the Spirit of God. These offer a great standard to measure whether a church is lined up with the purposes of God. What if you scored the effectiveness of your church by these five marks?

The Marks:

1. PASSION FOR JESUS: "When the operation is such to *raise their esteem of that Jesus* who was born of the Virgin, and was crucified without the gates of Jerusalem; and seems more to confirm and establish their minds in the truth of what the gospel declares to us of his being the Son of God, and the Saviour of men; is a sure sign that it is from the Spirit of God." Is Jesus the hero of your church? Is He the one who is most exalted, talked about, and worshiped?

Remember what Paul said to the Corinthians in I Corinthians 2? He told them when he came he did not come with the eloquent speech or the wisdom of men, but with the power of God and the Spirit. His message (v. 2) was Jesus Christ and His crucifixion. Matt Carter, Pastor of the Austin Stone Church he planted about ten years ago, went

completely against conventional wisdom when he planted
the church. Against the advice he received to use creativity to
reach a very liberal and unchurched Austin, Texas, he began
preaching Christ from the Gospel of John. For over four
years he went verse by verse through the Gospel. The Austin
Stone is a large, dynamic, gospel-driven church today
because of the focus on preaching the Word focused on
Christ. To hear more of Matt's story check out his message in
chapel at Southeastern Baptist Theological Seminary here:
http://apps.sebts.edu/multimedia/?p=3787.

Sometimes I think we do not talk to the lost about
Jesus because we do not talk to each other about him!

2. CONFRONTING IDOLS: "When the spirit that
is at work *operates against the interests of Satan's kingdom,*
which lies in encouraging and establishing sin, and
cherishing men's worldly lusts; this is a sure sign that it is a
true, and not a false spirit."

Throughout the Scripture when we read of times
God's people lost their vision and love for their God we also
see leaders confront their sin, and in particular their idols.
When a church faces decline and stands in need of
revitalization, leaders must confront the sin that stifles the
work of the gospel. We do have to be careful here, however,
because it is at this point where we must make two vital
issues clear: first, we must correct as shepherds who love
their sheep, not as taskmasters responding in frustration.
Second, we must be careful to confront the real issues. If we
confuse our personal preferences for unchanging biblical
truth and prioritize our wants over surrendering all for the
gospel, we may actually perpetuate the very reasons
revitalization is needed in the first place! I recently heard of a
pastor speaking at a conference in which he went on a fierce
rant against such issues as pastors who do not wear ties, or
preach on stools, or sing without hymnals. If these are the
issues of first priority to us, I have a pretty good idea why we
need to be revitalized.

I highly encourage you at this point to read Tim
Keller's book *Counterfeit Gods.* In this work he exposes the
reality of idolatry in our time and in our lives. He writes:

What is an idol? It is anything more important to you than God, anything that absorbs your heart and imagination more than God, anything you seek to give you what only God can give. A counterfeit god is anything so central and essential to your life that, should you lose it, your life would feel hardly worth living. An idol has such a controlling position in your heart that you can spend most of your passion and energy, your emotional and financial resources, on it without a second thought. It can be family and children, or career and making money, or achievement and critical acclaim, or saving "face" and social standing.[xxiv]

Are you constantly recognizing the idols in your community, your church, and your own heart? Are you confronting those idols with the gospel? Churches rarely move into stagnation and decline because they plunge headlong into gross sin. Often the reason churches lose a gospel vision is because good things become god things, and personal preferences matter – even in the church – more than the gospel. It would not be far off the mark to say that the reason most churches in America struggle stems from the idolatry rampant in the membership.

3. BIBLICAL TEACHING: "The spirit that operates in such a manner, *as to cause in men a greater regard to the Holy Scriptures,* and establishes them more in their truth and divinity, is certainly the Spirit of God."

Is the Bible taught clearly and without apology? Is the consistent teaching of Scripture a value in every ministry? Is the Bible taught more as a book of morality, or as a book of redemption? Is the Bible more valuable than politics, possessions, and position?

4. ADVANCING IN DISCIPLESHIP: "If by observing the manner of the operation of a spirit that is at work among a people, we see that *it operates as a spirit of truth, leading persons to truth,* convincing them of those things that are true, we may safely determine that it is a right and true spirit."

Do members value truth, even when it calls them to change? Are children taught to value truth, integrity, and honesty? Can people in the community see a difference in the believers among them? Are disciples of Jesus being created more than advocates of a Christian bubble?

5. INVEST IN THE CULTURE: "If the spirit that is at work among a people *operates as a spirit of love to God and man*, it is a sure sign that is the Spirit of God."

Do people in the community see your church as a valuable, caring part of the area? How do servers in restaurants talk about your church (that is a good, practical test of your love for a community)? Are members sharing the gospel verbally, but also investing in justice issues, like adoption and other real needs in the community?

A Helpful Book

I would encourage you to read in its entirety Edwards' work noted above called *The Distinguishing Marks*. You can find it for free online as well as many other books of Edwards. In addition to unpacking in more detail the five marks noted above, you will read his wisdom concerning those things which in themselves do not prove a movement is from God or not.

Warning: Edwards does not read like a comic book or a magazine. This is heavy lifting and takes careful reading. But like taking time to eat a thick steak, the work will be worth it.

Take Action:

Which of the marks noted in this chapter would your church align with currently? Which are in the greatest need of alignment?

Can you see how these marks could help a church to be revitalized as Edwards' church was?

Chapter Five
LEVERAGE: The Exponential Impact of Relationships

"As iron sharpens iron, so one man sharpens another." Prov. 27:17

As a college student I found myself often overwhelmed and unsure. I wanted to live for God, and I felt a call to ministry. I studied at a school where I learned the biblical languages and grappled with theological truth. But something was missing. Then I met Curtis Tanner.

Curtis Tanner was an athletic man who at the time dated a PE teacher at my university (and later married her). For reasons unknown to me to this day he asked me to join two other collegians for a weekly time of mentoring. That relationship grew me exponentially, multiplying the classroom training into daily living.

The work of leading a church in a revitalizing work is not for the faint of heart or the fly-by-night leader. You will need others to encourage you. And, the right people in your life can motivate you to see far more than you might dream. Do you have a mentor who exhibits a passionate, Christ-loving life, and effectively leads?

We Need Others

There are different types of mentoring for revitalization. As I have tried to illustrate, there are the historic mentors—the dead theologians society of past saints.

All my adult life I have read at least one biography of a great Christian annually. These have contributed incredibly to my passion for God.

You can have distant mentors, thanks to podcasts, books, and blogs. Find some men who push you, challenge you, and encourage you.

But more than anything, you need a Paul in your life, a man of God who can help you to stay focused as you lead.

Don't forget the other side of mentoring: you mentor someone else. Movements start with one who challenges the status quo and has early adopters or first followers. You may think the way to revitalize a church is to convince a large number or to have one service where the altar is filled. But it may be that one or two you mentor begin to catch the vision, and then they may influence others. Great awakenings did not happen because of the crowds but the committed few.

Beyond recording the events of Northampton and writing to defend the First Great Awakening, Jonathan Edwards mentioned other signs of revival he had discovered. He did so in the context of relationships:

> The Rev. William Tennent, a minister who seemed to have such things much at heart, told me of . . . a very considerable revival of religion . . . under the minister of his brother the Rev. Gilbert Tennent, and also at another place, under the ministry of a very pious young gentleman, a Dutch minister, whose name as I remember was Frelinghousa.[xxv]

The "Frelinghousa" he mentions is none other than Theodore Frelinghuysen mentioned earlier. These men encouraged one another. George Whitefield preached at Edwards' church and invited the Gilbert Tennent mentioned above to follow him as part of a preaching tour in New England.

Perhaps the idea of helping to step out in faith to lead in a revitalizing work frightens you. It should! This is a God-sized task and should bring us to our knees. But remember this: you are not alone. First and most importantly you have the Lord God to walk alongside you. The indwelling Holy

Spirit guides you. The gospel of the Lord Jesus Christ ignites you.

Enlisting Help Is a Sign of Strength Not Weakness

My friend and colleague Ken Keathley made a vital point about spiritual disciplines. We do not observe them to demonstrate our spiritual strength and superiority, he notes, but to demonstrate our weakness and our need for Christ. The wise leaders know they will never be able to lead in their own power and wisdom. They need both the power and wisdom of God and the help of others.

A young man named Chris Crain was called as pastor of the South Roebuck Baptist Church in Birmingham in his 20s. He has now been there 10 plus years. He sent me his church's story that I have summarized here. You can read it in detail at http://filesmynvc.org/Church%20Revitalization.pdf.

"Our church knew that Jesus said He would build His church and the gates of Hell would not prevail. Yet, we knew from our surroundings that an unloving response to the demographic changes of a transitioning community could cause death to prevail against our beloved church. God was at work. He was helping us to wake up to reality. . . . The churches in our area--many of them--had fought the good fight and finished the course; they have already ceased to exist as they once did. Other churches were relocated or 'transplanted' into new communities."

Chris sought help from others. He received helpful demographic information from New Orleans Baptist Theological Seminary and the North American Mission Board to help his people see the reality of their plight. The church realized it's need to change or die, and began a prayer focus on revitalization. Twenty-one key leaders began meeting to pray weekly.

Chris identified three keys:

    1. Respect the fact that they were an aging

congregation, and honor those who had remained. They would not relocate but start afresh with the core God had given them. But they also began a new focus of ministry. Sixteen members helped to start the North Valley campus in a growing community. In other words, they added without subtracting. This fed the second key:

2. Reach the next generation. The new campus proved to be effective in reaching young families in the area of growth.

3. Respond to a changing community. The community around the South Roebuck facility had changed remarkably. Once a home for Anglos, many African-American families now live closer to the mother church. They began a new ministry called South Roebuck Community Church, calling an African-American as pastor. "We share space, mission, theology, and resources," Crain observed. "We do not share the same strategies for reaching people or the same worship style. This shared diversity has been a good opportunity for people to reshape their views on race and stereotypes. People in both congregations are learning that humanity holds much more in common than they originally believed."

He summarized the challenges of a revitalizing work: "I would love to tell you that it has been easy to respect an aging congregation, reach the next generation, and respond to a changing neighborhood. Only in a dream world could there have been no hiccups along the way, no critics to hinder the progress, no regrets about things that could have been done differently. Reality paints a different picture. We have made mistakes along the way and have experienced numerous challenges. . . . Even after a time of 'success' things are still imperfect. We need more leaders. More money would help us try new ministries and reach out to new groups of people. I can tell you that even with all of the messes and misunderstandings, most of our people are glad that we did something! We didn't circle the wagons and die. South Roebuck Baptist Church was persistent about trying new things and reaching out to people with the Gospel."

Chris reminds others that while gaining help from others is critical, each place is unique:

"South Roebuck found no models to follow. No one was in our exact predicament. We couldn't pick up a kit at the local Christian bookstore to help us plan our way out of our declining status. We had no sister congregations who could lead the way for us. I can tell you that God was faithful to bring life out of what seemed to be death. He brought a zombie church to life again. We have arisen from our semi-comatose condition. We strengthened ourselves the best we could. We remembered the vision that planted us back in 1954. And, we are seeing God transform sinners into saints. Our baptistery is being used regularly again. Praise God!"

He describes the church today:

"Every Sunday we have five worship services stretched across two counties on two church campuses. I preach in three of those services. Two church planters preach in the other two. The Sunday worship services aren't large numerically. They are dynamic, each in their own way: each worship service rich with the presence of Jesus Christ; each service announcing the Gospel of the Savior Jesus Christ; each pointing to Jesus Christ as the way, the truth and the life."

Finally, he notes the ongoing nature of revitalization:

"Revitalization is not a one-time event. A church must be revitalized continually. It is my prayer that our story will inspire you to do something. Responding to the call of Jesus Christ to 'wake up strengthen what remains' is the responsibility of every church! What will your response be to the call of Jesus to church revitalization? Will you heed the call and open your spiritual ears to hear what could be done through your church?"

Revitalization is not easy. But it does not have to be lonely. Sometimes we may think of those lonely individuals who serve against all odds and (it may seem) all others. But wait: in the Bible, the overwhelming number of leaders who brought God's people to new places did not lead alone. Think about it:

--Abraham had Lot
--Moses had Aaron
--Joshua had Caleb
--King Saul had Samuel
--King David had Nathan
--Elijah had Elisha
--King Hezekiah had Isaiah
--Daniel had his friends
--Nehemiah had Esther
--Esther had Mordecai

Yes, Job stood alone, and Jonah as well. But more times than not God had a companion or more. Remember when Elijah was alone and complained to God? The Lord reminded him of 7,000 who had not bowed to Baal.

Often younger leaders had an older leader to guide them: Isaac had his dad Abraham, young Joshua had Moses, Samuel had Eli, a young David had Samuel, and so on.

> Another resource for revitalization: The Church Renewal Journey from the North American Mission Board -- http://churchrenewaljourney.net

In the New Testament Jesus had the twelve, and especially the three men Peter, James and John. Early in Acts you see Peter and John leading together. Look at all the companions Paul had from Barnabas to Luke to Silas and then young Timothy. We see modeled in Paul and Timothy the importance of younger leaders being guided by someone older, and we even refer to "Paul-Timothy" relationships because of their example. My point in this final chapter is simple: you do not need to lead a revitalizing work alone.

In high school a friend and I stood for Christ when ridiculed by fellow football players. We started a Christian club and eventually saw God do some cool things on our public school campus. Why? Because we did together what we probably would not have done alone. We encouraged each other in the tough times.

Pastor Randy Alston leads a typical congregation in the south. Not a large church, he came to serve this faith family after a season of long decline. He wrote me concerning factors that led to the beginning of revitalization in his church. In the following summary of keys for change you can see the impact of others in giving this pastor leverage for revitalization:

1. Alston intentionally sought out the advice of mentors, friends, and others. He knew this was a path he could not lead alone. While coming as a new pastor gave some initial momentum, he needed others.

2. He gave attention to expositional preaching with a focus on gospel recovery. He wrote: "I have recently realized that no matter where you are as a church you need to constantly be reminded of the gospel message of the death, burial, and resurrection of Jesus on behalf of sinners. I do not ever want our church to assume the gospel. I don't ever want to assume that everyone in my church fully understands the gospel. A recovery of the Biblical gospel is huge." A mentor helped in encouraging this consistent focus.

3. The church had mission trips going to the nations. Trips to India, Myanmar, Trinidad, Mexico, and Haiti have served both to get people to see a bigger vision of the world and to cultivate the pastor's relationship with members on these trips.

4. He mentors others. Although a young pastor, Alston began mentoring a deacon and teacher far past his age, but a man who had never been mentored. He also meets with two other men to grow together. One cannot revitalize a church from the pulpit only; he must invest in individual leaders, and he must be involved in the mission with them.

5. Seeing new people come to faith and new believers join the fellowship helped to add to the momentum.

6. The role of prayer. Some had prayed faithfully for many years, and the search committee that called Alston spoke often of their laboring in prayer. He is quick to note this: "God is doing a work. God is answering prayer. And these are prayers that have been going on for many years, by many people, at many times, in many ways, and in many places."

7. A few other practical areas: 1) Practical changes: they upgraded an out-of-date preschool area to be more inviting for young families. 2) The pastor was willing to confront difficult issues. One issue related to the role of music (it often does). The pastor faced accusations of everything from legalism to manipulation for not simply accepting the status quo, but he refrained from defending himself. This included a point in the life of the church where some key leaders needed to step forward and support the pastor, and by God's grace they did. 3) A willingness to subtract and to add. Some left the church, but more were added. After two decades of decline, the church has experience two years of consistent growth now. 4) When he preached in view of call for the church, Alston emphasized three areas on which he would focus: faithful preaching of the Word, reaching out with the gospel, and engaging the nations for Christ. He has been able to go back to these often.

He is quick to note they are early in the process and in a sense will always be in revitalization mode. But they find themselves in a wonderful season of God's blessing.

A Helpful Book

My eBook *With: A Practical Guide to Informal Mentoring* (NavPress Ebook) offers a simple way to be mentored and to mentor those who share a hunger for revitalization. It argues that involving mentees in every day life is the most effective way to learn from a mentor, as Jesus did with His disciples.

Take Action:

I would encourage you to listen to podcasts of pastors who have led their churches in revitalizing efforts. Some of these include J.D. Greear of Summit Church in Raleigh Durham, Johnny Hunt at First Baptist Church, Woodstock, Georgia, and Matt Chandler of Village Church in Dallas-Fort Worth.

CONCLUSION

Here is the reality: If you are a pastor or leader in some capacity in a local church or ministry, you *are* influencing others. Your influence matters, not just in the pulpit, but also in all of life. And God can use your influence to lead a revitalizing work.

Let me conclude by offering one practical place where your influence can greatly help or hinder the Lord's work of revitalization that has little to do with what happens in a church building: eating. You can tell a lot about a person in regards to how they eat. No, I am not referring to how much many of us eat (I have another book coming out that deals with this!). But make no mistake, our appetites and our actions around times of dining offer a practical reflection of our walk with Christ. In particular when we dine out, which is a significant part of life nowadays, how much we care for those around us is seen in our habits there.

Meals play a prominent role in the Gospels. Just this morning I read a couple of chapters in Mark, noting how fully half of the unique episodes in the narrative dealt with food and/or meals. The Gospel of Luke can hardly be understood without a careful examination of Jesus and meals.

Food matters in the biblical Story as well. What did God forbid Adam and Eve to do? Eat from one tree. What did God provide in the wilderness? Manna. What did Jesus share with His disciples soon before His death? The Last Supper. What will heaven be like? A wedding feast. My friend and colleague Tony Merida has built into the DNA of Imago Dei (the church plant he serves) the importance of hospitality. Specifically, this means meals with unbelieving friends. I regularly have a meal or coffee with friends who are at various stages of their spiritual journey.

I remind my students each semester of one of the best ways we can help those we lead to live missionally: simply watch how we act when we dine, specifically referring to dining out. The church honestly does not have a good reputation here. Just yesterday I received an email from a student about this subject. He saw in on the Facebook page of a friend who once sat in the same youth group he did but now has become another example of the dechurched. This young man remarked how he loathed serving on Sundays because of the church crowd, who would leave gospel tracts with cartoons about people burning in Hell instead of monetary tips.

The story to which this young man referred had to do with a pastor who refused to pay the auto-tip for a large group. Because the group had eight people in it the restaurant automatically added 18% as the gratuity, the normal practice. The pastor did not approve. The article quotes said pastor: "I give God 10%," the pastor wrote on the receipt, scratching out the automatic tip and scribbling in an emphatic "0" where the additional tip would be. "Why do you get 18?"[xxvi]

The pastor later admitted such actions brought shame to the church. But the question is, why would it take a waitress posting this on the Internet for a minister to get that this is not appropriate? My answer, in part: many of us live in such an isolated Christian bubble, surrounded by people who walk, talk, dress, and think like us, that we have virtually lost the ability to relate to people outside our world. As long as we sing praises to God and fulfill our church work, after all, we are good. Such a spirit will never revitalize a church.

Contrast the sad example above with one told by C.H. Spurgeon of a wife who emulated the love of Christ. Spurgeon comments:

A husband who was a very loose, depraved, man of the world, had a wife who for many years bore with his ridicule and unkindness, praying for him day and night, though no change came over him, except that he grew even more bold in sin. One night, being at a drunken feast with a number of his boon companions, he boasted that his wife would do anything he wished, she was as submissive as a lamb.

"Now," he said, "she has gone to bed hours ago; but if I take you all to my house at once she will get up and entertain you and make no complaint." "Not she," they said, and the matter ended in a bet, and away they went.

It was in the small hours of the night, but in a few minutes she was up, and remarked that she was glad that she had two chickens ready, and if they would wait a little she would soon have a supper spread for them. They waited, and before long, at that late hour, the table was spread, and she took her place at it as if it was quite an ordinary matter, acting the part of hostess with cheerfulness.

One of the company, touched in his better feelings, exclaimed, "Madam, we ought to apologize to you for intruding   upon you in this way, and at such an hour, but I am at a loss to understand how it is you receive us so cheerfully, for being a religious person you cannot approve of our conduct." Her reply was, "I and my husband were both formerly unconverted, but, by the grace of God, I am now a believer in the Lord Jesus. I have daily prayed for my husband, and I have done all I can to   bring him to a better mind, but as I see no change in him, I fear he will be lost for ever; and I have made up my mind to make him as happy as I can while he is here."

They went away, and her husband said, "Do you really think I shall be unhappy for ever?" "I fear so," said she, "I would to God you would repent and seek forgiveness." That night patience accomplished her desire. He was soon found with her on the way to heaven.

Spurgeon then drove home the point: "Yield on no point of principle, but in everything else be willing to bear reproach, and to be despised and mocked at for Christ's sake."[xxvii] If we cannot at something so simple as a meal show compassion and generosity to those who serve us, how can we tell others we love Christ who came not to be served, but to serve?

If across our great land servers began to see believers consistently go into restaurants with an heart of service, asking service how we can pray for them, showing kindness to them, tipping better than the minimum, and growing in relationships with the servers in our community, we might see many come to Christ. We might see churches revitalized. We might even see revival.

ABOUT THE AUTHOR

Alvin L. Reid (Born 1959) serves as Professor of Evangelism and Student Ministry at the Southeastern Baptist Theological Seminary, where he is the founding Bailey Smith Chair of Evangelism. A prolific author and speaker, Reid's books include *As You Go: Creating a Missional Culture of Gospel-Centered Students* (NavPress), *The Book of Matches* (NavPress, with Ashley M. Gorman), *With: A Practical Guide to Informal Mentoring* (NavPress), and *Evangelism Handbook: Biblical, Spiritual, Intentional, Missional* (Broadman & Holman), as well as others.

Reid enjoys spending time with his wife Michelle and their married children and their families. He also loves to exercise, read, and has a pet python named Lucinda.

To contact Alvin Reid for speaking on the subject of Revitalization please fill out the contact form at www.alvinreid.com.

Follow Alvin on twitter @alvinreid.

For more books available on the gospel see www.gospeladvancebooks.com.

Notes

---

[i] James Davison Hunter. *To Change the World: The Irony, Tragedy, and Possibility of Christianity in the Late Modern World* (Kindle Locations 617-621). Kindle Edition.

[ii] Gillies, *Accounts of Revival* (Quinta Press Reprint), 124.

and Influence in Baptist Life," *Review and Expositor* 77 (1980): 485-86.

[xvii]Ibid.

[xviii] Gillies, *Accounts of Revival*, 237.

[xix] Alexander Allen, *Jonathan Edwards* (Houghton Miffin), 134.

[xx] Ola Winslow, *Jonathan Edwards, 1703-1758* (New York: MacMillan, 1941), 134.

[xxi]Jonathan Edwards, "Sinners in the Hands of an Angry God," in *Complete Works*, II:10.

[xxii]Allen, *Jonathan Edwards*, 127.

[xxiii] "Memoirs of Jonathan Edwards," in *Complete Works*, I:lix.

[xxiv] Timothy Keller, *Counterfeit Gods: The Empty Promises of Money, Sex, and Power, and the Only Hope that Matters* (Penguin Group, 2009, Kindle Edition), Location 133.

[xxv] Jonathan Edwards, "Narrative of Surprising Conversions...,," in *Complete Works*, I:349.

[xxvi] http://news.yahoo.com/blogs/sideshow/applebees-waitress-fired-pastor-receipt-193820748.html (Accessed 2-1-2013).

[xxvii] http://www.spurgeon.org/sermons/1188.htm (Accessed 1-29-31).

Made in the USA
Charleston, SC
22 April 2013